Heart of Texas
A Lone Star ABC

By Laura Krauss Melmed

Illustrated by Frané Lessac

Collins

An Imprint of HarperCollinsPublishers

Alamo

Here brave troops displayed their courage
When they vowed to take a stand
To win liberty for Texas
Under Travis's command.
And though woefully outnumbered,
Facing Santa Anna's might,
They chose never to surrender
As they waged their valiant fight.

Three million people visit
the Alamo every year—
more than any other
famous place in Texas.

The word "Alamo"
means cottonwood
tree in Spanish. The
Alamo was built by
Spanish priests in the
1700s as a religious
mission, when Texas
belonged to Mexico.

Davy Crockett was a famed
pioneer, soldier, trapper,
explorer, and congressman
from Tennessee. He
volunteered to fight at the
Alamo, along with his twelve
sharpshooters, the "Tennessee
Boys." Crockett called his
trusty rifle "Old Betsy." Besides
being a crack shot, he
entertained everyone inside
the Alamo with his wild stories
and fiddle playing.

DAVY CROCKETT

JIM BOWIE

Jim Bowie, a well-
known soldier and
pioneer, was named
first co-commander at
the Alamo with William
Travis. But Bowie fell
sick on the second day
of the siege and turned
over full command to
Travis. Although
bedridden, Bowie
stayed at the Alamo
and was killed there.

In 1836, Texans were fighting for independence from Mexico. To stop them, Mexican General Antonio López de Santa Anna marched his army of 5,000 men toward San Antonio. As they neared, Colonel William B. Travis led about 200 Texas fighters to the Alamo, an empty set of buildings behind a wall. The Texans held out against heavy attacks for thirteen days. On March 6, Mexican troops breached the walls and a bloody battle left all the Texas defenders dead.

Legend says Colonel Travis drew a line on the ground, asking any man willing to stay and fight to step over it. All but one crossed over. He was Louis Rose, a Frenchman who had been an officer in Napoleon's army.

For most of the siege, townspeople traveled freely in and out of the Alamo. There were women and children staying inside the walls, but none were harmed.

Forty-six days after the Battle of the Alamo, General Sam Houston led his men to the Battle of San Jacinto. Shouting "Remember the Alamo!" 783 Texans beat 1,500 Mexicans in less than twenty minutes. While only nine Texans lost their lives, 630 Mexican soldiers were killed and 730 were taken prisoner. General Santa Anna, disguised as a peasant, was captured the next day. Texas independence had been won!

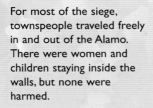

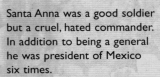

Santa Anna was a good soldier but a cruel, hated commander. In addition to being a general he was president of Mexico six times.

SANTA ANNA

Big Bend National Park

Rushing river, rugged canyons,
Dusty desert, mountains tall,
Burly bears and lurking lions,
Big Bend Park has got them all.

Hike a rocky trail or bird-watch,
Raft the rapids or canoe,
Climb a mountain peak and marvel
At the never-ending view.

Big Bend National Park was created in 1944 by an Act of Congress signed by President Franklin D. Roosevelt.

There are about 24 mountain lions living in the park. Visitors and park employees report lion sightings about 150 times a year.

Fossils found in the park include a shellfish three feet wide and four feet long, the largest known pterosaur (a flying dinosaur), and the skull of a chasmosaurus, a horned dinosaur.

From 145 million to 65 million years ago a great inland sea covered most of West Texas. Countless skeletons of sea creatures sank into the lime mud on the seafloor and slowly hardened into limestone rock. Then the sea dried up. For millions of years since, the river has been wearing down the limestone, creating the looming canyons of Big Bend.

Big Bend is named for the great U-turn made by the Rio Grande here as it flows north for some miles.

Who lives in Big Bend? There are 450 different types of birds, 75 types of mammals, and 67 types of amphibians and reptiles.

The golden eagle's body is about three feet long. Its wingspan is six to eight feet, at least twice the size of its body. (A person's arm span and height are usually about equal.)

The jackrabbit's large ears are an early warning system for predators. The ears also act like an air-conditioner by releasing body heat.

The Great Blue Heron is a wading bird.

Archaeologists have found proof that humans were living in the Big Bend area at least 10,000 years ago.

The park covers 1,250 square miles, about the area of Rhode Island. It includes parts of the Rio Grande and the Chihuahuan Desert, and all of the Chisos Mountains.

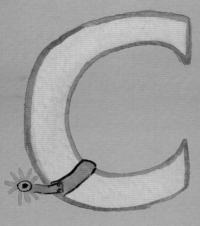

Cowgirl Museum and Hall of Fame, Fort Worth

They were pioneers and artists,
Stars of rodeo and screen,
Fearless girls who tamed wild stallions
Fast as any horse you've seen.
From O'Keeffe to Annie Oakley
This museum shows the best
Of the women who embody
The bold spirit of the West.

The cowgirl of frontier days found new freedom in riding across the wide-open spaces of the West. Life was hard, but there were many rewards. Other women of the American West followed the cowgirl's model of bravery and strength. The National Cowgirl Museum and Hall of Fame tells their stories.

ANNIE OAKLEY

Annie Oakley (1860–1926) started hunting as a child to support her widowed mother and family. She grew up to become a sharp-shooting superstar, performing all over the world. With a shot from her rifle, Annie could split a playing card in half from ninety feet away and then put five or six more holes in it before it hit the ground!

Coming into the Greatest Rides exhibit is like entering a rodeo arena. Three swinging screens rotate like the gates of a rodeo chute. They show movies of the greatest women riders in American history.

The Hall of Fame honors women ranchers, rodeo stars, authors, artists like Georgia O'Keeffe, a WW II pilot, a Supreme Court justice, a Native American tribal head, and many other amazing women.

The museum has more than 3,000 photographs of Western women and their lives, starting from pioneer times until today. In the museum's library, there are books, original letters, diaries, and scrapbooks.

How long can you hang on? The mechanical bucking bronco will take you for the ride of your life! A video of your performance can be later downloaded to your computer.

On the outer wall of the museum is a trompe l'œil (trick of the eye) mural in which five cowgirls on horseback seem to be galloping right at you at top speed.

Dallas Cowboys

They are Cowboys without horses
For pro football is their game.
Wearing white and blue and silver
They have scored their way to fame.
And a roar goes up like thunder
At their home games or away
As the fans cheer on the Cowboys
While they execute each play.

Team members wear silver helmets, silver pants, and either white or blue jerseys. Some fans have decided that the blue away jerseys must be jinxed because the team often loses when wearing them.

Rowdy, the Cowboy's official mascot, drives onto the field on his four-wheeler, tosses T-shirts into the stands, holds up signs that say "Let's Go, Cowboys!", and makes fun of the opposing team.

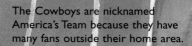

The Cowboys are nicknamed America's Team because they have many fans outside their home area.

Cowboy players in the Hall of Fame include Super Bowl quarterback Roger Staubach, tackle Bob Lilly, and running back Tony Dorsett.

The team was formed in 1960. It is part of the National Football League. For years, the Cowboys' home was Texas Stadium in Irving, Texas, outside Dallas. But in 2009 the team moved to a new stadium in Arlington.

DALLAS COWBOYS SUPER BOWL WINS

Game Number	Date	Opposing Team	Score
VI (6)	1972	Miami Dolphins	24–3
XII (12)	1978	Denver Broncos	27–10
XXVII (27)	1993	Buffalo Bills	52–17
XXVIII (28)	1994	Buffalo Bills	30–13
XXX (30)	1996	Pittsburgh Steelers	27–17

Tom Landry was the team's first head coach, from 1960 to 1988. Landry was famous for developing new plays. He was inducted into the Pro Football Hall of Fame in 1990.

The team reached the playoffs for eight years in a row from 1966 through 1973 and for nine years in a row from 1975 to 1983.

Unlike many NFL teams, the Cowboys do not retire jersey numbers of outstanding past players. Instead, the team places their names in a "Ring of Honor" that encircles the field.

COWBOYS

Enchanted Rock

This immense pink dome of granite
Is a rock of lofty height.
Legend says it might be haunted,
For it sometimes creaks at night.
You can climb it, then go camping
In the huge surrounding park—
It's the perfect place to picnic
And to stargaze after dark.

Enchanted Rock is in the Texas Hill Country, south of Austin, Texas. It is thought to be one billion years old. The aboveground dome of pink granite covers 640 acres. It is part of a much larger underground formation of about 90 square miles (around the size of the city of Amarillo).

The park is good for seeing stars because there are no nearby streetlights, or lights from towns or cities, to compete with the stars.

There are over 500 types of plants in the park. One rare tropical fern grows only here and in out-of-the-way parts of Florida. In spring there are beautiful wildflowers such as bluebells and Indian paintbrush.

Long ago, local Indians believed that a Spanish conquistador got lost here and put a spell on the Rock. The Indians thought they saw ghost fires flickering at the top of Enchanted Rock. They heard the Rock creaking and groaning at night. Today geologists say this is caused by the sun-heated Rock contracting, or shrinking, as it cools off at night.

Please don't eat the rocks! Rock formations scattered about the park are shaped like donuts or mushrooms.

Animals that live here include armadillos, rabbits, deer, squirrels, and lizards.

Fiestas Patrias, Houston

He was called Father Hidalgo,
And he made a heartfelt plea
To end Spanish domination
And help Mexico go free.

Now the call for liberation
That this daring priest once made
Is a cause for celebration
With a party and parade.

There are many Mexican-American, or Tejano, people who live in Texas. To show pride in their way of life and Mexican heritage they celebrate a September holiday called Fiestas Patrias. There is special music, dancing, food, shows, and costumes. In Houston, Fiestas Patrias lasts the whole month of September.

It was 1873 and Fort Worth was about to get its first railroad. B. B. Paddock, a young newspaper editor, imagined a map with Fort Worth in the center and rails spreading in all directions. When he published it, people thought it looked like a spider and called it the Tarantula Railroad, although it had nine legs, not eight. In time the railroad did spread out from Fort Worth in all directions. Today the railway is called the Grapevine Historic Railroad.

The Grapevine Railroad follows the old Chisholm Trail. This trail was used by cowboys from 1867 to 1884 to drive cattle and mustang horses to Kansas to be loaded onto railcars.

There is also a 1953 locomotive that runs on diesel fuel. The train cars are from the 1920s.

Puffy, or Steam Locomotive No. 2248, is a ten-wheeler built in 1896. After many steam engines were replaced by diesels, Puffy was converted by the Southern Pacific Railroad to a fire control "pumper" locomotive to fight forest and tunnel fires in Northern California. Puffy later was used in railroad ceremonies before being sent to Fort Worth.

Today the Grapevine Railroad takes visitors from the Stockyards Station in Fort Worth, along the route of the Chisholm Trail, to the Cotton Belt Depot in Grapevine, Texas. Grapevine is an old town with many buildings restored to the way they looked in the late 1800s. The city is named for the wild mustang grapes that grow in the area.

University of Texas, Austin

A vast school of higher learning
Almost fifty thousand strong,
White and orange are its colors,
"Eyes of Texas" is its song,
And its campus is in Austin,
Home to barbecue and bats,
Music clubs and politicians,
Business suits and cowboy hats.

School mascot: Bevo,
the Texas Longhorn

The university's first football game was in 1893. The first game between UT, Austin and its biggest rival, Texas A&M University, took place in 1894. In 1955 a cheerleader named Harley Clark taught fans the famous "Hook 'em Horns" hand signal. It has been used ever since at Texas Longhorn football games and as a greeting by UT students and graduates.

Founded in 1883, the campus is more than 350 acres (or almost 300 football fields put together).

The Tower atop the Main Building can be seen from all over the campus. It is 307 feet high, about the same height as the Statue of Liberty.

There are fifty-six bells in the Kniker Carillon on top of the Tower. A carillon is a set of at least twenty-three bells sounded by clappers. The bells are played by a bell ringer using a keyboard and foot pedals. Every fifteen minutes the bells peal the four notes known as the Westminster Chime. On the hour, the largest bell sounds.

The Tower is lit with orange and white lights for sports victories, holidays, and special events such as graduation.

There are seventeen libraries on campus, including the LBJ Library holding the papers of President Lyndon Baines Johnson. Altogether the UT libraries contain eight million books.

Father Miguel Hidalgo y Costillo was a Mexican priest now known as the father of his nation. In September of 1810, Father Hidalgo was the first to call for poor Mexicans to rise up against the Spanish. His brave cry, or *grito*, set off the Mexican Revolution. Mexican Independence Day, or El Diez y Seis de Septiembre, is celebrated on September 16 in his honor.

FATHER HIDALGO

Hundreds of thousands of cheering Houstonites turn out during the fabulous Fiestas Patrias parade. Traditional dancers of the Ballet Folkórico in dazzling costumes whirl down city streets to Mexican music. Marching bands and drill teams strut their stuff. The parade ends with the crowning of Miss Fiestas Patrias.

Galveston's Strand

It was once the business center
Of a booming Texas town—
Then a storm of crushing power
Almost brought the city down.
But the people built a seawall
As a shield from future harm
And restored the fine old buildings
To their former Southern charm.

Galveston was a booming port throughout the 1800s, especially for shipping cotton. The Strand, where most of the businesses were located, was called the "Wall Street of the Southwest." This ended after the Great Storm of 1900 hit.

The Great Storm of 1900 was the fiercest hurricane ever to hit the United States, including Hurricane Katrina. On September 8, 1900, the winds raged through Galveston at 140 miles per hour. More than 6,000 people (one out of every five) lost their lives. There was severe flooding and damage to homes and other buildings.

The city of Galveston is on a barrier reef island, a ridge of coral or rock running beside a coastline. Galveston is separated from Houston by Galveston Bay.

The island was once home to the Karankawa and Akokisa Indians. Spanish explorer Álvar Núñez Cabeza de Vaca, captured by the Karankawa in 1528, became a healer and trader while living with them.

Does your city have a beach? Galveston has thirty-two miles of them!

Many people walk, skate, or ride bikes along the seawall, which stretches out for ten miles.

After the storm the people of Galveston worked hard to rebuild. Over the next eight years, they raised the height of the land up to twenty feet with sand pumped from Galveston Bay. Little by little they built a seawall for future protection. When another strong hurricane hit in 1915, there was little damage.

Famous architects gather in Galveston every summer. They compete to see who can build the most amazing sandcastle or sand sculpture.

The Strand

GALVESTON ISLAND TROLLEY

502

502

Famed pirate Jean Lafitte lived in Galveston in the early 1800s. His combination house and fort was called Maison Rouge (Red House) after the color he painted it.

You're aboard a NASA shuttle
As it hurtles toward the stars,
On a space walk, floating weightless,
Or controlling probes on Mars—
At Kids Space Place, Blast Off Theater,
Or on Johnson Center tours,
When your mind is on space travel
Your imagination soars!

The city of Houston was named for Sam Houston, military leader, hero, and first elected president of the Texas Republic. It's the largest city in Texas and fourth largest in the United States.

NASA is the U.S. space agency. Its Lyndon B. Johnson Space Center is where scientists and other workers design and test spacecraft and is the home base for astronauts. Space Center Houston is the visitors' center, offering exciting chances to learn about the past, present, and future of space exploration.

At Blast Off Theater visitors feel the thrill of launching into space—from the rocket boosters to the billowing exhaust.

On the NASA Tram Tour, visitors may go to the Historic Mission Control Center, the Space Vehicle Mockup Facility, or the current Mission Control Center. They may even get to see astronauts training.

Nearly 300 people have flown in space since the first Mercury rocket took off in 1961.

The Astronaut Gallery has the world's best collections of spacesuits worn by astronauts. There are photos of every astronaut who ever flew into space.

The Starship Gallery holds spacecraft and equipment going back to the beginning of man's journey into space, including the *Gemini V* spacecraft; a lunar roving Vehicle Trainer; the *Apollo 17* Command Module; and the giant Skylab Trainer.

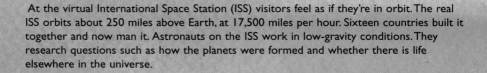

At the virtual International Space Station (ISS) visitors feel as if they're in orbit. The real ISS orbits about 250 miles above Earth, at 17,500 miles per hour. Sixteen countries built it together and now man it. Astronauts on the ISS work in low-gravity conditions. They research questions such as how the planets were formed and whether there is life elsewhere in the universe.

Island

There's an island known as Padre,
Long and narrow as a spear—
You can water-ski or kayak,
Search for shells, or windsurf here.
Make a visit to the lighthouse
Or just swim and play and doze
Until ghost crabs skitter past you
As the day draws to a close.

Padre Island is one of 300 islands stretching from Maine to Mexico. These natural barrier islands help protect the mainland from storm damage. Padre sits off the coast of Texas in the Gulf of Mexico.

The island is about 130 miles long. It has the longest sand beach in the United States. A huge sand dune runs along the shoreline for more than 100 miles. The central part of the island is a wild nature preserve called Padre Island National Seashore.

Off the central part of the island lies the 12,000-foot-deep Sigsbee Deep, the deepest part of the Gulf of Mexico.

Laguna Madre is the shallow, enclosed waterway between Padre Island and the coast of Texas.

Nests from five of the world's seven sea turtle species have been found at Padre Island. They are leatherback, hawksbill, green, loggerhead, and Kemp's Ridley. All are now either threatened or endangered. The division of Sea Turtle Science and Recovery is working to protect these turtle populations so they will grow larger.

Blacktailed jackrabbits, ground squirrels, gophers, kangaroo rats, coyotes, and Eastern moles are among the many mammals found on the grassy areas of the island.

Herons, ibis, egrets, spoonbills, pelicans, cormorants, ducks, and geese use the island and the lagoons as a sanctuary and breeding ground.

The island is home to thousands of beach animals such as clams, crabs, sea urchins, and sand dollars. Most live in sand tunnels or burrows and are hard to find.

Visitors to Padre Island from April through July can watch turtle hatchlings being released.

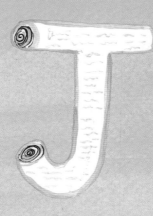

Juneteenth Festival

Lincoln made a proclamation
Back in 1863
Saying slavery was outlawed
And all people must go free.
But for slaves who lived in Texas
It took years before they heard—
Now the Juneteenth celebrations
Mark the month they got the word.

On January 1, 1863, two years before the end of the Civil War, President Lincoln signed the Emancipation Proclamation freeing the slaves. But it wasn't until June 19, 1865, when Union General Gordon Granger read the proclamation in Galveston, that the slaves of Texas were freed. Juneteenth is a remembrance of this historic day.

Juneteenth is celebrated with family gatherings, picnics, parades, rodeos, fishing, baseball, blues festivals, and dancing. Speakers and elders in the community talk about the past, present, and future of the African-American people.

Special treats to enjoy on Juneteenth include barbecue and strawberry soda.

It seems hard to believe that it took more than two years for the news to reach Texas. An old folktale says the man carrying the news rode the whole way to Texas on a slow-as-molasses mule. Some historians believe that the slave owners may have actually kept the news of freedom from their slaves.

Little Miss Juneteenth Pageant

For years former slaves and their families returned to Galveston on June 19 to celebrate. Little by little the Juneteenth celebration, as it came to be called, spread to other places.

Today this festival takes place all around the United States and in other parts of the world. It honors African-American freedom, education, and all that African Americans have accomplished.

Kennedy Memorial/ Sixth Floor Museum

A shot rang out in Dallas—
A president was slain.
A nation watched in horror,
Then wept in shock and pain.
This museum tells what happened
That sad and fateful day
And helps the world remember
The life of JFK.

Kennedy created the Peace Corps. It sends Americans to developing countries to help with education, farming, health care, and construction.

Kennedy set a goal of "landing a man on the Moon and returning him safely to the Earth" during the 1960s. The Apollo 11 mission did this in July 1969.

John F. Kennedy was president of the United States from 1961 until 1963. Lyndon Johnson, a Texan, was his vice president. In Kennedy's first speech as president he said, "Ask not what your country can do for you; ask what you can do for your country."

John F. Kennedy and his wife, Jacqueline, known as "Jackie," were very young compared to earlier presidents and First Ladies. They were very popular with the American people. With their two young children, Caroline and John Jr., they made the White House a lively place. It even had a preschool and a tree house.

Kennedy wanted to help the young and the old by improving education and making sure the elderly had medical care. He promised an end to racial discrimination. Congress voted in these programs after Kennedy's death, when Johnson was president.

JOHN F. KENNEDY

To celebrate the greatness of America, the Kennedys hosted American artists, writers, scientists, poets, musicians, actors, Nobel Prize winners, and athletes at the White House.

On November 22, 1963, President Kennedy was shot and killed while riding in a car through Dealey Plaza in Dallas. Crime investigators figured out that the shots were fired from a window on the sixth floor of the Texas Book Depository building.

Lee Harvey Oswald was arrested for the assassination. In a horrifying twist, Oswald himself was shot to death less than two days later, in a Dallas police station by Jack Ruby.

Some people wanted the Texas Book Depository torn down. Instead, the Dallas County government created a museum and memorial to President Kennedy on the sixth floor. Here, visitors can learn about Kennedy's life and times, the contributions he made, his death, and what this tragedy meant to the United States and the world.

Longhorn Trail

Oh, the story of the Chisholm
Is a long and dusty tale
Of three hundred thousand longhorns
Herded yearly on that trail.
Boss and wrangler, cook and cowboy
Drove those cattle north and then
Said good-bye to them in Kansas
And rode south to start again.

After the Civil War, Americans began to eat more beef than ever before. To meet the demand, over five million longhorns were driven, or "trailed," from Texas along the Chisholm Trail between 1867 and 1884. At rail yards in Kansas they were loaded onto trains and shipped north and east, where they brought ten times the price they fetched in Texas.

The Longhorn breed grew from a mix of Spanish and English cattle. The horns of older longhorns are often wider from tip to tip than a man is tall. Ranchers liked longhorns because they thrived on just water and grass. But these cattle were also half-wild and had a bad temper.

Ranchers let their longhorns run free on the open range. Cattle from many ranches grazed together. To keep track, each ranch had its own symbol or brand marked onto the calves' skin with a hot branding iron.

A cattle drive on the Chisholm Trail took two to three months. It was dusty, dangerous work. There were six rivers to cross, plus many creeks, canyons, and low mountain ranges. There might be rustlers (cattle thieves) or unfriendly Indians. Sometimes the longhorns would break into a stampede.

A cattle-trailing group of cowboys was called an outfit. Each outfit had about eighteen men and 100 mustang horses. During a cattle drive they would trail from 2,000 to 3,500 cattle.

The Trail Boss was in charge. Several times a day he would ride miles ahead of the herd to check on rivers and grazing areas. He often had to break up fights among the other cowboys.

The cook, often called Cookie, drove the chuck wagon. He prepared three meals a day for everyone. A typical menu might be steak, beans, sourdough biscuits, and dried apple pie.

After barbed wire was invented, ranchers had a way to fence cattle in. But longhorns were not well suited to this. By the 1920s only a few longhorns remained. People sent some longhorns to wildlife refuges and Texas state parks. After a while, cattlemen began to buy the longhorns again, so the breed lives on.

The first cattle drivers to use the route drove a herd of 2,400 animals to Kansas following wagon tracks made by a part-Cherokee man named Jesse Chisholm. Chisholm was a trader who traveled back and forth to Indian camps with supplies. The trail was later named for him.

Missions, San Antonio

To convert the native Texans,
Catholic priests were sent from Spain,
And together they built missions
That to this day still remain.
From this meeting of two cultures
That began so long ago
Grew the fascinating city
Known as San Antonio.

Beginning in 1718, a group of Catholic priests was sent to settle in the territory of New Spain near the San Antonio River. The priests' job was to convert the local Indians to the Spanish way of life.

Together the priests and Indians built five walled missions. Inside the walls were a church and a cemetery. There were rooms for the Indian families to live in and workshops where they learned crafts such as weaving and wood carving. Outside the walls were orchards or small gardens called *huertas*. Beyond these were the *labores*, fields for growing crops such as corn and chiles. Even farther away were the ranches where cattle, horses, sheep, and goats were raised by Indian *vaqueros* or cowboys.

On the Feast Day of Saint Anthony in 1691, in what is now central Texas, some Spanish explorers and missionaries came upon a river. They named it San Antonio in honor of the saint. The Indian name for this same river was *Yanaguana*, meaning clear or refreshing waters.

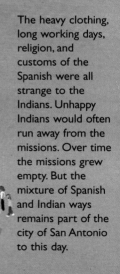

The heavy clothing, long working days, religion, and customs of the Spanish were all strange to the Indians. Unhappy Indians would often run away from the missions. Over time the missions grew empty. But the mixture of Spanish and Indian ways remains part of the city of San Antonio to this day.

Today visitors can tour all five missions. The most famous is Mission San Antonio de Valero, which became known as the Alamo. The others are Mission San Jose, Mission Concepción, Mission San Juan, and Mission Espada. Those four are now part of San Antonio Missions National Historical Park.

In the mid-1800s Sam Houston, first president of the new Republic of Texas, wanted to build towns, farms, and businesses. He called upon people from Europe to settle in Texas. Many came from Germany.

In 1845 a German prince, Carl of Solms-Braunfels, brought over a boatload of German farmers and craftsmen. Leading them in a wagon train to the middle of Texas, the Prince purchased many acres of farm land. The settlers built farms, stores, mills, and workshops, calling their town New Braunfels. It was soon a booming market town.

Schlitterbahn is the name of a water park in New Braunfels. The word means "slide."

Wurst means "sausage" in German. Every fall New Braunfels holds Wurstfest, a ten-day celebration of German heritage.

Little by little German settlers moved out to other parts of Texas, especially around the center of the state. Today about 18 percent of Texans have German ancestors.

Tejano music was created in Texas and spread all over the world. Selena was its most popular singer. It is a mixture of traditional Mexican music styles with German accordion music. Tejano music sounds like country music performed in Spanish to a polka beat.

Yum! Texas barbecue! German settlers loved to eat smoked meats and sausage. At lunchtime, butchers would sell smoked meat on sheets of butcher paper to farmworkers at the back door of their shops. Texas barbecue was born!

New Braunfels

German families came to Texas
And they stayed to stake their claims,
Building towns such as New Braunfels
That still carry German names.

Now in music, food, and culture
German influence abounds,
As in Schlitterbahn and Wurstfest
And Tejano's blended sounds.

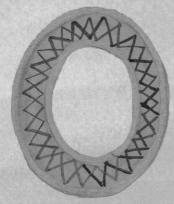

Oil Wells

Tales of Spindletop in Texas
Through the years have been retold:
How a man whose name was Higgins
Drilled the earth and hit black gold.

Other drillers came a-rushin',
And as more and more was found,
They rejoiced to see their fortune
Come a-gushin' from the ground.

Crude oil is a smelly, yellow-to-black liquid usually found in underground areas called reservoirs. Scientists and engineers choose a drilling site by studying rock samples. Above the drilling hole, a derrick is built to house the tools and pipes going into the well. The well will bring a steady flow of oil to the surface.

In 1899, geologists said there was little chance of finding oil in the salt domes of the Texas Gulf Coast. But Patillo Higgins and Anthony Lucas bored a hole in an underground salt dome at Spindletop, in east Texas. On January 10, 1901, a noise like cannon fire boomed from the hole. Out gushed oil, higher than an eighteen-story building—more oil than anyone had ever seen before. The Texas oil boom was on!

After Spindletop, thousands of drillers rushed to probe Texas for "black gold." This scramble created the huge oil companies we now know as Exxon, Texaco, and Chevron.

The word "petroleum" comes from the Latin *petra*, or rock, and *oleum*, or oil. Oil was formed millions of years ago, before the dinosaurs, from the remains of sea animals and plants. Over the years, the remains were covered by layers of mud. Heat and intense pressure turned them into what today we call crude oil.

Texas produces more oil than any other state. The other four biggest oil states are Alaska, California, Louisiana, and New Mexico. More than one fourth of crude oil produced in the United States comes from offshore drilling in the Gulf of Mexico.

Spanish explorers used the black, sticky tar that washed up on beaches along the Texas shore to waterproof their boots.

The amount of crude oil produced in the United States gets smaller each year. But our use of products made from crude oil keeps growing. That is why the United States buys more than half of its crude oil and petroleum products from other countries.

Exploring and drilling for oil may disturb land and ocean habitats. But technologies such as satellites, global positioning systems, and remote sensing devices now find oil reserves while drilling fewer wells. In the "rig-to-reefs" program, old offshore oil rigs are toppled and left on the seafloor to become habitats for sea creatures.

Crude oil is sent by pipeline, ship, or barge to a factory called a refinery. There, it is separated into products such as gasoline, diesel fuel, jet fuel, and heating oil. Petroleum is used to make crayons and bubble gum, deodorant, eyeglasses, tires, artificial heart valves, and many, many other products.

Oil is measured in barrels. Have you seen a gallon of milk or water? A barrel holds forty-two times that much crude oil.

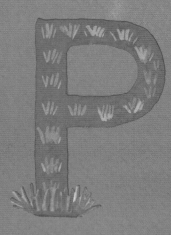

Panhandle

Some compare this part of Texas
To the handle of a pan.
Its vast miles of rolling grassland
Have been changed by modern man.
Now on land where hunters wandered
And the longhorns rambled free
You'll find cities, farms, and ranches
Where wild spaces used to be.

The Panhandle makes up the northernmost part of Texas. It is shaped like a handle on the "pan" of Texas. The Panhandle includes the High Plains, the Rolling Plains, and between them a 250-mile-long cliff called the Caprock.

In 1541 Spanish explorer Francisco Vásquez Coronado was the first European to cross the High Plains. He was followed by settlers who started ranches and farms.

The Indians of the High Plains depended on buffalo hunting. But white hunters killed the buffalo by the thousands and sent their valuable skins back east. The buffalo were soon wiped out and the Indians became very poor.

In 1874, led by Comanche Chief Quanah Parker, the Indians attacked the whites, leading to the Red River War against the U.S. Army. The Indians were defeated and forced onto reservations, ending an entire way of life for the Southern Plains tribes.

Amarillo is the largest city in the Panhandle. Palo Duro Canyon, southeast of Amarillo, is the second-largest canyon in the United States.

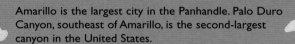

In the Panhandle, scientists have found mammoth carcasses along with weapons used to kill them and tools used to scrape their hides. Some date back to 9200 BCE. They were left by the Clovis people, ancestors of such Indian tribes as the Kiowa and Comanche.

Charles Goodnight started the Panhandle cattle industry when he settled there with 1,600 head of cattle. Goodnight also invented the chuck wagon, which carried food and cooking equipment on the prairies of North America.

There are fourteen Quarter Horse colors, including black, bay (reddish-brown with a black mane and tail), palomino (cream), and gray. There are no white Quarter Horses.

The Quarter Horse was a powerful short-distance racer, or sprinter. It got its name from the popular quarter-mile horse races held on the streets of Colonial towns. During the American Revolution Quarter Horses carried soldiers and supplies between colonies.

During the 1800s vast cattle ranches began to stretch across Texas and other Western states. The Quarter Horse, known for its cow sense, or ability to work with cattle, and its calm ways, became the ideal working ranch horse. It was especially skilled at cutting, or separating an animal from the rest of the herd for branding or other reasons.

Cow horses were often called "Steel Dusts" after a legendary horse named Steel Dust who won several famous races before an injury ended his career. After this, many horses were bred from Steel Dust. These speedy horses were sought by cowboys.

Today Texas has the most American Quarter Horses of any state.

The American Quarter Horse is a mix of the Thoroughbred racehorse, brought over in Colonial times from England, and the Chickasaw Indian horse descended from the horses of Spanish conquerors.

The Quarter Horse helped the pioneers move West by pulling their wagons.

Quarter Horse Museum

Much beloved by cowboy, cowgirl,
Racehorse owner, pioneer,
This fine steed known as Steel Dust
Helped to settle the frontier.
From a working horse to show horse
To a racer of great speed—
It's the Quarter Horse of Texas,
A most legendary breed!

The American Quarter Horse Heritage Center and Museum is in Amarillo. It has a Quarter Horse skeleton, an authentic chuck wagon, and a talking horse. Visitors can learn about prehistoric horses, modern racing, rodeos, and members of the Quarter Horse Hall of Fame.

Swift and nimble, Quarter Horses are used in rodeo events such as barrel racing and roping.

The Quarter Horse is still the most popular racehorse next to the Thoroughbred.

In 1836, Texas was part of Mexico but wanted independence. On March 1, while Texans were battling the Mexican army in the Texas Revolution, fifty-nine delegates gathered in the town of Washington-on-the-Brazos. They declared Texas independent and wrote a constitution. The Republic of Texas was born!

The three elected presidents of the Republic were Sam Houston, Mirabeau B. Lamar, and Anson Jones.

Republic of Texas

Fighting Mexico for freedom
Texas finally stood alone,
With one star upon its banner,
As a country of its own.
Nine years after independence
Texas joined the USA.
And the Lone Star waves on proudly
Over Texas to this day.

On the Lone Star flag, the blue stands for loyalty, the white for purity, and the red for bravery. The Lone Star flag is one of six that have flown over Texas, including the flags of Spain, France, Mexico, the Confederacy, and the United States.

The Republic faced constant threats of war with Mexico and lack of money. Texans knew joining the United States would bring protection and funds. The United States admitted Texas as the twenty-eighth state on December 29, 1845.

For their capital city the Texas Congress chose empty land on the banks of the Colorado River. The new city was named Austin after renowned Texas statesman Stephen F. Austin. The Texas government moved to its new home in October 1839. The capitol building in use today is the largest of any state capitol. It is built of Texas pink granite and was completed in 1888.

Southwestern Exposition

Bronco ridin', ropin', wrestlin'—
It takes bravery and skill
To perform the feats of daring
To which audiences thrill.

The Southwestern Exposition—
Pull your boots on and let's go
To a genuine, rip-roarin',
Rootin', tootin' rodeo!

The Southwestern Exposition and Livestock Show in Fort Worth has been held every year since 1896. It has the oldest running rodeo in the United States. There is also a carnival, a Mexican celebration, a petting zoo, and sales of ranching equipment, clothing, and many other items.

Cowboys wear wide-brimmed hats to protect them from sun and weather, tall-topped boots with slanted heels to help keep their feet in the stirrups, and pointed spurs to urge on their horses.

The word "rodeo" comes from a Spanish word meaning roundup. In the days of the open range, cowboys rounded up the cattle to brand and count them. For fun they would challenge one another to ride untamed horses, called broncos. A cowboy could win by riding the bronco until it stopped bucking. If the cowboy hit the dirt, the horse won. When someone started charging money for people to watch these contests, the sport of rodeo was born.

Rodeo events such as barrel racing and riding broncos and bulls are based on cowboy skills. The first cowboys were Spanish-speaking *vaqueros* (sometimes called buckaroos) from Mexico and the southwestern United States. They taught the English-speaking newcomers the riding and roping skills needed for controlling cattle.

Rodeo clowns act very funny, but their job is really to protect bull riders. When a rider is in trouble the clown draws the bull's attention. This gives the cowboy time to run for safety.

The Moos Brothers, two seven-foot-tall bulls named Hoss and Elwood, are the mascots of the Exposition.

In the calf scramble kids try to catch calves on the run.

The Stock Show gives awards for the best beef and dairy cattle, horses, mules, donkeys, pigs, sheep, goats, llamas, chickens, pigeons, and rabbits.

Train

Once this railway line was nicknamed
For a hairy, scary bug.
But don't worry, you won't see one
When old Puffy starts to chug.
From the stockyards to Old Grapevine
And along the Chisholm Trail
Let the Grapevine Railroad take you
To the Old West via rail.

The Fort Worth stockyards were once a center for the cattle industry. Today at the stockyards you can buy Western gear like a saddle or cowboy boots, watch a rodeo, or eat in one of many restaurants. There's a cattle drive twice a day, as cowboys move a herd of longhorn cattle down Exchange Street. A funny man riding a longhorn steer may let you sit on it and take a picture.

Austin has many
music clubs and
barbecue
restaurants.

Austin is the capital of Texas. It was named after Stephen F. Austin (1793–1836), "the Father of Texas." As a young man Austin persuaded Mexico to provide cheap land to settlers from the United States and brought more than 6,000 Americans to Texas. The capitol building in Austin is the largest state capitol in the U.S.

The nightly journey of more than one million bats from under the Congress Street bridge is a famous sight in Austin.

Viva El Paso!

It's the story of El Paso
Told in drama, song, and dance—
Tales of gunfights, priests, explorers,
Cattle rustlers, and romance.
From a Wild West trading outpost
To the city that we know,
You'll see history unfolding
At this starlit outdoor show.

El Paso is called Sun City because the sun shines there about 302 days out of 365 per year.

The city of El Paso sits at the far western tip of Texas on the banks of the Rio Grande.

In 1682 Tigua Indians and Spanish settlers founded Ysleta del Sur Pueblo, the oldest settlement in Texas. Later the city of El Paso grew around it.

Viva El Paso! is Spanish for *Hurray for El Paso!* It is a show performed in McKelligon Canyon on summer nights, at a theater carved into the Franklin Mountains. In song, dance, and drama, it tells the story of how Native American, Spanish, and Western American people settled the city of El Paso.

People lived in the El Paso region for thousands of years before the first Europeans came. In 1581 Spanish conquistadors came upon the Rio Grande from the south. They saw two mountain ranges rising out of the desert with a deep split, or mountain pass, between them. Because of this they named the place El Paso del Rio del Norte.

In 1849 the U.S. Army opened Fort Bliss near El Paso. The troops there defended the border with Mexico and maintained law and order. They protected settlers and pioneers. They also surveyed for the new transcontinental railroad. Fort Bliss is still a large and important army post.

In 1881 the Southern Pacific Railroad opened in El Paso. It linked El Paso with the rest of the U.S. and with Mexico. Newcomers streamed in. Soon the town was a wild place filled with gunfighters, cattle rustlers, saloons, U.S. marshals, and Texas Rangers. As businesses grew, new laws were passed and El Paso became a large, modern city.

Ciudad Juárez just across the river in Mexico is El Paso's sister city.

Wildflowers, Lady Bird Johnson Wildflower Center

She was wife to Lyndon Johnson
And she wanted to ensure
That our country's natural beauty
Would exist forevermore.
As you ramble through her gardens
Bright and blooming, you will see
What a precious gift this Lady
Has bestowed on you and me.

The Lady Bird Johnson Wildflower Center is in the Texas Hill Country near Austin. It has many gardens filled with plants and flowers that grow wild in the United States. Visitors learn how to respect and care for the plants. Experts from all over the country use the center as a place to share information about the natural world.

The Texas bluebonnet is the official state flower. In the 1930s the Texas Highway Department planted bluebonnets along most major highways. They bloom in late March and early April.

The Little House Courtyard and Garden at the Center is a small, special place where kids can play and learn.

Wildflowers often have funny or poetic names. In the Texas Hill Country alone you can find Green Dragon, Old Man's Beard, Scrambled Eggs, Frog Fruit, Sneezeweed, Skeleton-Plant, and many more.

Lyndon Baines Johnson (LBJ) became vice president to John F. Kennedy in 1960. On November 22, 1963, when Kennedy was shot and killed in Dallas, LBJ was sworn in as president. He was elected president in his own right in 1964.

Mrs. Johnson's given first name was Claudia. It is thought that when she was a tiny girl, her nanny gave her the nickname Lady Bird. She was called that her whole life.

Lady Bird Johnson was the wife of Lyndon B. Johnson, 36th president of the United States. The Johnsons were both born and raised in Texas. As first lady traveling around the U.S. Mrs. Johnson saw that cities and roads were taking over the forest, seashore, and desert, so she helped pass laws to keep the wild areas protected by creating national parks. She had flowers planted along the highways as well as thousands of tulip and daffodil bulbs in Washington, D.C. In 1984 Mrs. Johnson received the Congressional Gold Medal for helping to make America beautiful.

LADY BIRD JOHNSON

On her seventieth birthday in 1982, Mrs. Johnson gave the United States money and land to start the National Wildflower Research Center. On her eighty-fifth birthday the center was renamed in her honor.

LYNDON B. JOHNSON

TeXas State Fair

As you know if you're from Texas,
Everything is BIGGER there,
Like BIG Tex, the GIANT cowboy,
Who will greet you at the fair.

Yup! The BIG state fair of Texas,
With its twenty-four-day run,
Is where folks throng by the millions
For a HEAP of Texas fun.

"Ho-w-w-w-w-d-e-e-e, folks! Welcome to the State Fair of Texas!" Big Tex, a fifty-two-foot talking cowboy figure, greets fairgoers at the center of the grounds. He sports a seventy-five-gallon cowboy hat and his boots are seven and a half feet tall.

The fair is held every fall in Dallas for twenty-four days.

At the fair you will find amusement rides and games, livestock shows, cooking contests, art competitions, outdoor musical events, IMAX films, concerts, a car show, museums, demonstrations and crafts, singers, dancers, magicians, yummy food to eat, and more.

The fair was first held in 1886. Thousands of folks came to view prizewinning cattle, ride in a hot-air balloon, inspect the latest in farm machinery, or bet on a horse race. There were concerts, and contests for the best cakes, pies, jams, jellies, and needlework. Broadway shows came to Texas for the first time to play in the magnificent Music Hall.

Three U.S. presidents have visited the fair: William Howard Taft, Woodrow Wilson, and Richard Nixon. The fair closed during World War I when the grounds were used as a temporary army camp and again during World War II.

Dallas is the third largest city in Texas after Houston and San Antonio.

The Texas-Oklahoma football game is one of the biggest rivalries in college football. It has been played every year since 1929 at the Cotton Bowl during the Texas State Fair.

Ysleta Pueblo

Pueblo dwellers called the Tigua
Settled here and made a home.
And they built Ysleta Mission
With its shining silver dome.

They have many old traditions
That they once were forced to hide
But that now they're free to practice
With much dignity and pride.

Near Ysleta in the Chihuahuan Desert is the Hueco Tanks State Historic Site. Here rock basins fill up with water from rare desert rainfall and underground springs. For thousands of years people came here to gather water and to hunt. They left paintings on the rocks. Over 2,000 of these, called pictographs, are still there. For the Tigua, Hueco Tanks is a sacred place.

Spanish missionaries and Tigua Indians fleeing from a Pueblo Indian war in New Mexico started Ysleta del Sur Pueblo on the banks of the Rio Grande in 1681. Ysleta is the oldest community in Texas. It is now part of the city of El Paso.

The Ysleta Mission stands in the center of the community. The church is a very important place of worship for the community. The Tigua also practice their native religious ceremonies.

For hundreds of years the Tigua tried to claim the land they lived on, but they were not accepted by the U.S. government as a tribe. In 1968 President Johnson signed an act of Congress recognizing the Tigua tribe and making their land a reservation.

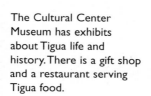

The Cultural Center Museum has exhibits about Tigua life and history. There is a gift shop and a restaurant serving Tigua food.

At the Splash! exhibit, located in a pretend limestone cave, visitors find out how the Edwards Aquifer was formed. They guide a virtual drop of water through the cycle that creates Barton Springs. Through displays of the endangered Barton Springs salamander and other water animals, they learn how important it is to keep our springs, creeks, and rivers clean.

There are playgrounds, baseball, football, soccer, and rugby fields, canoes for paddling on Town Lake, an Asian garden with waterfalls and a teahouse, a rose garden, a butterfly trail, a xeriscape garden with plants that need very little water, and a small pioneer village.

"All aboard!" The Zilker Zephyr train has been carrying passengers on the three-mile trips along Barton Creek to Town Lake and back for more than fifty years.

At the Annual Austin Kite Festival in March, hundreds of homebuilt kites fill the sky above the park.

The Nature and Science Center has a living nature museum. Injured and orphaned animals are cared for here. There is a birds of prey aviary. An eighty-acre nature preserve has trails and wild caves.

At the Dino Pit visitors can dig for fossil casts modeled on actual fossils found in Texas. There are real dinosaur tracks believed to have been made 100 million years ago by an ostrich-like dinosaur, ornithomimus. The shell of a large sea turtle, osteopygis, was discovered here and is on display.

The Barton Springs swimming pool is nearly 1,000 feet long (an Olympic-size pool is "only" about 164 feet long). It is filled with natural spring water from a huge underground water source called the Edwards Aquifer. Every day, 27 million gallons of chilly, 68-degree water comes pumping out of the main spring under the diving board.

Zilker Park, Austin

Grab your bathing suit and towel,
Then dive in and splash around
In a giant pool of water
Pumping out from underground.
Toss a Frisbee or go caving,
Try your hand at making rain,
Or explore the park while riding
On the Zephyr mini-train.

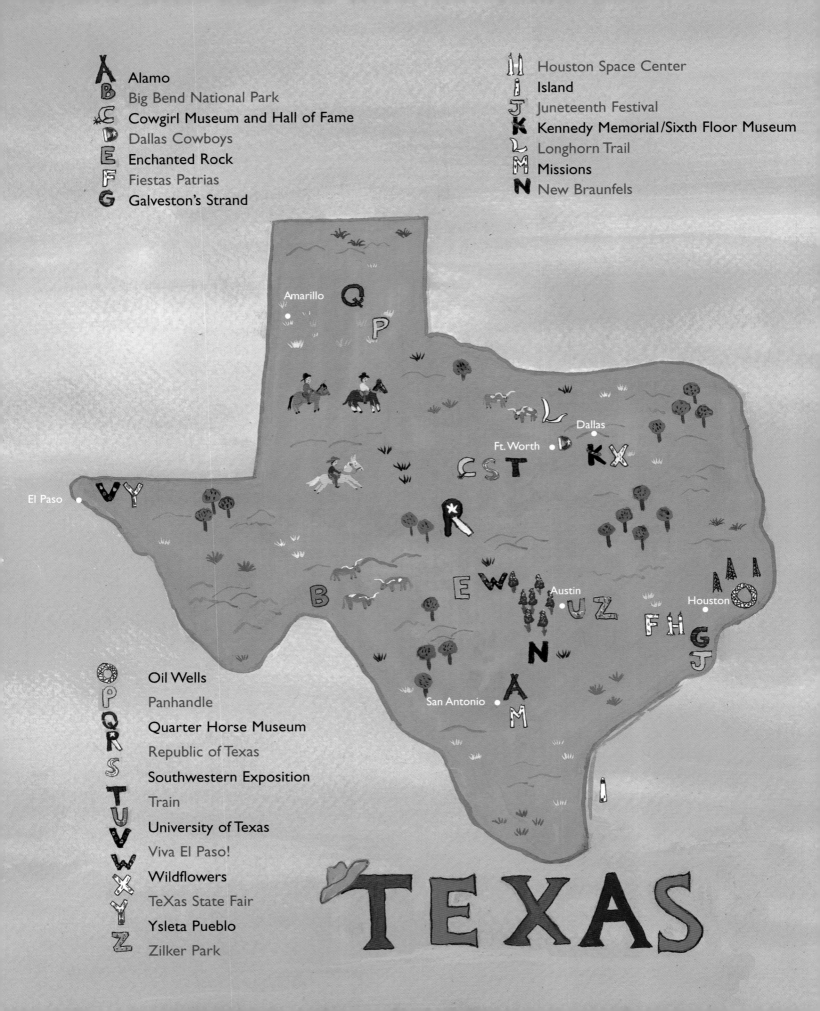

A Alamo
B Big Bend National Park
C Cowgirl Museum and Hall of Fame
D Dallas Cowboys
E Enchanted Rock
F Fiestas Patrias
G Galveston's Strand

H Houston Space Center
I Island
J Juneteenth Festival
K Kennedy Memorial/Sixth Floor Museum
L Longhorn Trail
M Missions
N New Braunfels

O Oil Wells
P Panhandle
Q Quarter Horse Museum
R Republic of Texas
S Southwestern Exposition
T Train
U University of Texas
V Viva El Paso!
W Wildflowers
X TeXas State Fair
Y Ysleta Pueblo
Z Zilker Park

Amarillo

El Paso

Dallas
Ft. Worth

Austin

Houston

San Antonio

TEXAS